STORY STRUCTURE AND MASTER CHAPTER OUTLINE © WORKBOOK

Other books by C. MICHELLE JEFFERIES

Chrysalis Series

LATENT 0

ASCENSION 1

INTERLUDE 1.5

CONVERGENCE 2

CATALYST 3

STORY STRUCTURE AND MASTER CHAPTER OUTLINE © WORKBOOK

by C. MICHELLE JEFFERIES

STORY STRUCTURE AND MASTER

CHAPTER OUTLINE © WORKBOOK

ISBN: **978-1974175444**

Edited by Meraki Books
Cover Design by Meraki Books

To Lauri, who believed so hard in my system that I believed in it too.

STORY STRUCTURE & MASTER CHAPTER OUTLINE WORKBOOK

If found please return to:
Author name:

Address:

Phone #:

Email:

Basic Outlining and Structure

Many people have expressed frustration about structure and outlining. They say it's too complicated, or that by outlining something in great detail, they've already essentially written the book and the newness of the discovery phase is lost and there's no desire to write the book anymore. That structure takes away the organic feel of writing. That the fun of writing is lost when they are expected to follow a guideline.

I hope to remedy that.

There are many styles of structure, plotting and outlining. They are all good for different people. I myself use the seven-point structure as described and used by such people as Larry Brooks author of many books including "Story Architecture", and the website storyfix.com, and Dan Wells author of "I Am Not A Serial Killer." I am also going to give you insight into my own master chapter outline system which I developed as I wrote and then edited and revised my first book Emergence and then again with Latent.

There is a certain freedom and thrill in pantsing a book. The allowing the characters to do whatever they want to do is appealing and the discovery phase is often times thrilling as an author to use. The problem in pantsing is, unless you're really intuitive about the direction the story is going and needs to go, the story can wander all over the world or book. This can be a problem when you get to the middle or the end of the book and you find that the book is sagging in the middle or that the book has no clear resolution or satisfaction in plot or character.

This is where simple outlines and structure come into play. It allows the writer to have a lot of freedom in what happens in the story while providing a skeleton that can be used as a basis for the story. I often times draw an analogy between using structure and making muffins. You need certain ingredients in certain amounts at certain times. Like flour, oil, binder, leavening, and sweetener. However, like muffins, structure and basic outlining allows you to choose what type of story detail or ingredient you choose. Whether you use whole wheat flour or white, sugar or honey. Whether you write romance or horror, every genre can benefit from structure and outlining.

First, we should cover the basics.

What genre is the story you want to write? It's okay to blend genres as long as you understand the rules regarding genre. Your story should have a major genre. Such as romance, suspense, or dystopian. Then if you so choose, add a sub-genre. Do you like suspense but want some romance in it? Great then it's romantic suspense. Horror with deeper characterization and less gore. Then it's light horror. Fantasy with a more modern twist? Urban Fantasy.

For our story, we're going to analyze structure and outline for Latent which is a suspense since that is what I know best.

What is the genre of your story?

Once you have decided genre it's most likely time to create a working title. Don't like titling your book so early in the process? Fine, it's not needed, but often times a title gives you as the writer a feel of what the story is about. It doesn't have to be a long drawn out process either. Sometimes titles change in the middle of a book.

Ideas for a title?

So now that, that is decided, we choose a setting. Usually, in suspense, we have the normal world and there's something threatening that world or the characters specifically. It's different than a romance in the respect that there's more at stake than just whether the guy gets the girl. Not that you can't have romance in it. But that's not the focus of the story. The focus is the character who lives in the normal world and must protect themselves and family and friends from the antagonist or the world from the antagonist.

So what is in your setting? This is a moment where detail whether the reader ever sees all of them or not is important.

A good story is only as good as the setting plot and characters.

Next is characters. We need the good guy here after is known as the protagonist. And we need the bad guy who is known as the antagonist. Keep in mind the antagonist can be amorphous. It can be nature, an animal, a machine, the protagonist's noble self-desires, or inner demons. Or it can actually be a separate real life living breathing creature.

Who are your characters? Your protagonist? Your antagonist? The most important question here about character is why. Why is he good? Why is he bad? Why is the antagonist bad and it can't just be because. There has to not only be redeemable characteristics for the antagonist, but also reasons as to why they think they are the good guy and thinks he has a noble purpose. Same goes with the protagonist, he can't be perfect. He has to be human and have flaws believable ones and he has to be teachable and approachable. Yet, he can't be too flawed as well. The reader needs to care about the character in the first chapter. Or there's no reason to turn the page and read chapter 2.

Character is sometimes hard to get but once you understand it, it becomes ingrained and becomes a lot easier.

So the protagonist in my story is Antony Danic. An atheist assassin, retired military, with a lot of inner demons and strong opinions.

The antagonist is a few people. First, Mitsuo Damashii, Mr. Kurosaki, Maiko Damashii, the man in black glasses, and Sori Katsu. Last and the most important part of the antagonists is Antony himself. He creates the hardest scenarios for himself. He imagines and creates by action and reaction the most impossible hills for himself to overcome. The basic theme of this story is "man VS himself". We need this because, in order to be who he is by the end of the story, he needs to have the doubts, fears, inabilities, and deconstruct himself on his own.

There are faults and inner demons he faces. And there are quirks that he owns and creates to deepen those inner conflicts and stakes. His unique behaviors make the reader resonate with the protagonist.

Who is your protagonist?

Antagonist?

Secondary characters?

Next comes the nitty gritty part of basic structure. Concept and theme. And believe me, they are different. Lets tackle theme first, the easier to understand. Theme is the feel of the book and the repeating elements that make the story cohesive. The recurring themes in the story are how the story is presented and how it feels. For example, in a historical novel, the costume and setting is styled in period dress and is as accurate as possible. For our story, the theme is creating a believable future without letting the setting and technology overshadow the characters.

What is your theme?

Concept is harder. It's the big story question and it's not necessarily that what if question. It's way beyond that. Concept is the question or idea that makes your story huge and different than other people's stories. For my story, the concept is what does it take to change a bad boy to a good guy.

What is your concept? Dig deep here. The deeper the concept the better the story.

Once the basics are decided we move on to the actual storyline. We need a few things in the basic storyline.

A beginning and end.

Who is your protagonist?

What does he want?

Why?

Where do you want the protagonist to be by the end of the story?

What does the antagonist want?

How do the protagonist and antagonist oppose each other?

We need the parts of the story which becomes the basis for character arc for all main characters and the antagonist.

Parts of Story:

Introduction - Beginning to Plot Point 1

Protagonist's life, and setting established. This section describes the old and ordinary world that the protagonist lives in at the beginning of the story. It gives the writer the chance to create resonance between the reader and protagonist so when things start to happen to the characters the reader cares enough to follow the story.

Reactive Stage - Plot Point 1 to Mid Point

"What the heck happened?" The first plot point creates a moment of change, whether big or small internal or external that changes the protagonist. It puts the protagonist on the edge of the old and new worlds. They then have a choice to refuse to move on, (which then the story dies) to choose to move into the world with a sense of adventure, or dread because of trauma, or is forced into the world because the old world is permanently changed and unlivable (for the protagonist) because of trauma or disaster. The reaction stage is the protagonist reacting to that move into the new world. Everything is new and different. They gain friends, mentors and allies and new information. They are still reacting so the friends and information result in more fail cycles than successes.

Active Stage - Mid Point to Plot Point 2

"Not on my watch!" (or "oh no you didn't just point that gun at me.") The Mid Point changes Everything and the protagonist has to move from wanderer with a few ideas to a warrior with plans. This is where he slowly loses friends and allies, gains more info, starts to succeed in his plans, and by the end of the action stage is ready to face his personal demons and the antagonist and defeat them.

Resolution - Plot Point 2 to End of Book

Coming home, tie up all ends. The hero must emerge and protagonist engages as the primary catalyst. The hero must conquer their inner demons and show personal growth. Ending of the book should resonate with the readers.

In addition to the plot parts of the story, there is a notion that your protagonist can go through character arc traits that describe some of the what and why of the characters progress throughout the story. Below is a list of the character parts as they relate to the plot parts.

This list is from the author and book: Carol S. Pearson The Hero Within: Six Archetypes We Live By

Orphan
Lacks direction, lives in ordinary world
Wanderer
Reacting to PP1, moving but no plan
Warrior
Reacting to MP, has clear plan, building to PP2
Martyr
PP2 and beyond, willing to sacrifice, becomes hero

One thing to note, the main plot conflict should be resolved right around plot point 2 or the moment when the protagonist and the plot move from reaction stage to resolution stage. Don't put the conflict and the character change in the middle of the resolution stage. The reader will most likely be dissatisfied with the end of the book and you don't want that.

Plot Points

Plot points are the defining moments in the story.

They are supposed to happen at the quarter marks in the story, IE PP1 at 1/4th the way into the story.

However, if they don't happen at exactly the proposed time or aren't just one scene, that's okay. I myself tend to have really short resolution stages and long mid points.

The first point in the story is called the Hook.

It happens early in the story, preferably the first few chapters.

It:

Gives the reader some clue as to the conflict later in the story.

Provides some action or conflict in the introduction part of the story.

The next point is called Plot Point 1.

It happens at 1/4 the way through the story. It begins the reaction stage of the story, and the wanderer character stage.

It is:

Most important part of your story.

The protagonist's call to action, or event that starts everything moving.

The true introduction of the conflict.

After this point, the protagonist or Hero's life can never be the same.

Can be external or internal.

Doesn't have to be dark and earth-shattering.

An essential element of Structure is Pinch Points.
They:

Are a reminder of the conflict and bad guy throughout the story.

Should happen at least once halfway between PP1 and MP and once between

MP and PP2.

Can be sprinkled throughout the story. Deepens the conflict, and raises the stakes.

The next Point is Mid Point, it is crucial to a good story.

It marks the middle of the book and heralds in the active stage for the characters. This is where your character goes from wanderer to warrior.

It:

Can be a huge unexpected twist in the story leaving the characters and reader shocked, or

something so subtle the protagonist doesn't even know that things have changed. (but reader does)

New information that changes the experience and understanding of the protagonist,

the reader or both.

Changes the protagonist from reactive stage to active stage

Prevents the "sagging middle"

The last plot point is Plot Point 2

It happens at about 3/4 through the book and is where things wrap up and we move from active stage to resolution stage and where the character goes from warrior to martyr.

It is:

The climax of the story. "The final car chase scene."

New information or something happens that takes the protagonist toward the conclusion of the story. The story shifts into resolution mode. No new info, or characters after this point

Structure for Romance Writers:

Part one - Introduction: This is the normal world your couple lives in.

Theme introduction: The couple either meets for a brief moment or passes each other at a future familiar place.

Plot Point #1: Couple meets and there's emotion happening.

Part two - Reactive Stage: Romance blooms only to be robbed from them by something.

Pinch Point #1: The couple can't be together for some reason

Mid Point: They decide against all odds that they want to be together.

Part three - Proactive Stage: They make plans and start acting proactively.

Pinch Point #2: Another setback. Will they ever get together?

Plot Point #2: The final meeting, rescue, accidental bumping into each other and confess their love.

Part four - Resolution: The characters have their Happily Ever After

Where does the outlining come in?

Right here.

I have the belief that you can't outline and write a story without at least a simple structure. They are cohesive and go hand in hand.

So how do we approach this Master Chapter Outline? It's actually really simple. The coolest thing is that if you do it the way I describe it, you have a workable synopsis at the end of the planning stage as well.

This is where we stop the instructions and I'm going to ask you to get a few things.

A pen or pencil.

Some highlighters.

Strips of paper, post-it notes, or index cards and some tape.

A large section of wall, a door, or a large table.

Some time.

Remember the parts and plot points we talked about on the previous page?

These are your placeholders while the actual story ideas are the elements that move you away from those points and toward the next point. This is where the skeleton and the discovery part of writing collide into something beautiful, that is not only adaptable to your tastes but workable in every story. Because no story is going to hold to the EXACT formula every time. Otherwise, the stories would all become formulaic.

While there are some people that think that the main points should happen on an exact page, I think that kind of thinking limits us in creativity. There's nothing wrong with a point or two coming early or late or one part of the story being shorter or longer than the others.

In Latent the reaction stage is longer than the action stage. The plot midpoint is six chapters long. The character arc midpoint is late in the story. The resolution is short. Do any of them happen right at the right point? Yes, plot point one is almost exactly at the suggested spot. The midpoint happens in the middle of the book the resolution is at the end. But is it exact? Nope. The story dictated where things happened. Not a milestone or a page number.

So the beginning, like any good story or movie we begin not at the beginning but in a place where for a moment at least we can see the main character in what they consider the normal world. This introduction stage should last about ¼ of the book. Sometimes it is shorter, that's okay. If you are writing fantasy you're going to be doing a lot of world-building at this stage and it's okay to go long as long as things are happening to your characters. If you are writing other genres you cannot go too long in the ordinary world. The reader will close the book and maybe even throw it. That's not good.

On at least one of your pieces of paper, you need to write down what the ordinary world is for the protagonist. These don't have to be drawn out or detailed. In fact, I find that too much detail kills my muse and then I lose the desire to write the story. Where are we when we first meet him or her? What are they doing?

Certain things need to happen in this introductory stage. You need to hook the reader. This means that some event needs to happen to the protagonist that gives the reader a hint of the conflict that happens later in the story.

In Latent the hook is Antony's argument with the street preacher, establishing that he's an atheist and the religious conflict in the story and his need to get home to something solid in his life, which is Elite.

You need to write on a separate piece of paper what events happen that take the protagonist from this introductory moment in the first chapter to the hook. Each scene should be on a separate piece of paper and we'll get to why later. In the scenes leading up to the hook and away from the hook there should be hints as to the antagonistic force and the conflict.

I'm not saying to give it all away. Just make the characters, world, and conflict so interesting that the reader can't put the book down. Make the protagonist and antagonist so resonant that they care about them by page five, ten, or thirty. Is this the easiest thing? Oh no, it is hard. But it's also a learned technique, meaning, learn it now and it becomes like muscle memory. Much easier to do the next time.

One note to remember, often times the scenes that build up to a point, (scene) and the scenes that lead us away and toward the next point (sequel) are usually three scenes long. For a writer like me where each scene is a chapter, it means that the three chapters before and after the point are leading up to and then away. This is also in character arc the time where the protagonist is usually making plans and then reacting to the plans either succeeding or failing. This is also called a try and fail cycle.

This intro stage is also where we get to meet and see the other characters and the antagonist, at least briefly. If your story has ANY romance in it at all you need to introduce the other romantic interest character(s) in these first pages.

So at this point in time, you should have the introduction, the protagonist's ordinary world, the scenes leading up to the hook, and away from the hook on separate pieces of paper. You should also have scenes where the other characters and the antagonist are introduced. Don't worry about order right now. That happens later as well. Just get them on paper. Another thing that is a good idea right now i.e. to write why this scene is relevant and moves either plot or character on the paper as well.

One thing I like to do at this point is start to color code the cards the protagonist gets one color, the love interest or other characters another, the antagonist yet another color and then scenes that relate to the points another color. This little tool helps you to see when everything is out in the open where you are lacking in one or another element and it helps you keep it balanced.

So we hit the hook. This is that point in the story where we see a hint of what is going to happen later in the book. It doesn't have to be big, it can be internal or it can be very large and leaves the reader reeling and you haven't even hit plot point one.

Remember that if your hook is huge that the other plot points need to be as big or bigger. So my suggestion especially if this is one of your first books, that you keep the large stuff for the midpoint and plot point two.

Once we've hit the hook part we move toward the first plot point. There needs to be some reflecting and thought process about the hook as the protagonist moves forward. Remember we're still establishing the normal world. If we move too fast into the plot point one then we either have a novella-length beginning or we have this horrible long middle that has no choice but to sag because of timing. So give us scenes that are interesting, that establish the world and characters and start building up to the introduction of the real conflict that is plot point one. Each scene we think of needs its own piece of paper or card.

(I buy tons of index cards at back to school time they're about 50 cents a pack at this time.)

Another note. DO NOT NUMBER YOUR SCENES OR CARDS AT THIS POINT IN TIME. HOWEVER, DO

LABEL THEIR PARTS OR POINTS. IE HOOK, INTRO, ANTAGONIST INTRO etc.

Another note: there doesn't need to only be one point of conflict in the beginning of the story, in fact, I think this is a good time to introduce the character quirks inner demons and internal conflict. As well as setting conflict and other character and plot details.

Don't make it a laundry list but give little things to the reader that make the character setting and conflict resonate with the reader. Is your character afraid of spiders? This would be a great time to have a moment with one in the shower for example. Or are they afraid of speaking in public? Make them give a short spiel about introducing themselves to a group of strangers.

Antony loves to fade into the background, so to be the object of attention is uncomfortable. Which is why when he and the street preacher collide he is even more irritated than normal because he is sure people are watching him. And in his head, the assassin needs to be invisible.

Make sure it's relevant and that these quirks can be used against them later in the story or something that is conquered as a moment of strength and growth later. In our story Antony hates crowds, he hates being exposed and he hates feeling out of control. In the wedding scene where another preacher reveals they know he's an assassin it starts that unraveling process and throws Antony into a panic attack which not only makes him the center of attention, he can't control what's happening to his body and it makes it worse.

Plot point one is actually called many things in the plotting world. It is the call to action, the inciting incident, or the movement moment. This is the incident where the protagonist's normal world disintegrates right in front of them. This is the incident that forces the character to move forward. Because looking back there's nothing left for them in the old world. And to go back will result in unhappiness or the feeling of not belonging anymore. Granted the character can refuse to move for a short period of time and the uncomfortable(ness) or irrelevant(ness) of the old world is then what forces them to move forward. There's nothing left for them there.

From this point in time, there are two separate things happening to them and the story. There's the move from the plot point one to the midpoint which in the plot is the gathering allies and making plans and the strengthening the antagonist stage. In the character arc, it is the reaction stage. Where the character thinks, "what the heck just happened?"

This is the stage where all of the try/fail cycles are mostly failing. And while the protagonist is gathering allies and making plans, the antagonist is acting bold and is gathering minions and making plans and executing plans as well.

Do not allow your protagonist to fail all of the time it only leads to frustration in the reader's mind and again they are tempted to close, throw or burn the book. The protagonist has to succeed a little and he has to make some inner demon strides while still appearing vulnerable and appealing. The antagonist has to be cunning and determined and his plans and motives must be not only reasonable but in some ways almost redeemable.

So at this point, we should have cards of scenes leading away from the hook, towards plot point one and from plot point one toward midpoint. We need to see protagonist reactions, antagonist actions, gathering of allies, and minions, and plans made executed, and successes and failures.

In Latent, the plot point is the death threat to Elite at the church in Canberra. It throws him from the normal world into one where he begins to suspect everything from Maiko and Damashii Enterprises, to his own ability to protect Elite and himself. As well as protect the children at the orphanage who he has grown to love.

Enter the midpoint. The all-important weapon against the sagging middle and the death of a lot of stories. Mid point is the most important point in the story in my own personal belief. This is that moment where we take the protagonist who is struggling and reacting and failing in his plans and make him active and a move him from wanderer to warrior.

Midpoint can be subtle or big, but it needs to be profound no matter how we write it. Sometimes the protagonist doesn't even know it happened but senses the shift in their favor and that alone changes the reactive stage to the active stage. Sometimes the protagonist sees the midpoint and that changes their mode of operation.

This is the point where new information is revealed that changes everything. Something happens to the protagonist that makes everyone including the reader have an "A-ha" moment. This is where twists happen. Where people reveal their true colors or betrayal hits the protagonist. This point often leaves the protagonist reeling and they react sometimes violently, but also physically and emotionally. Often times the midpoint has a really active build up and an equally emotional reaction to it. Whatever you do, make it equal and don't overdo it unless you have a blockbuster conflict resolution scene. I often refer to this point as the "Oh no, you didn't just point that gun at me." stage.

This is the moment in the book where the protagonist starts to act on the plans made and while he has gathered his allies, he slowly loses them to betrayal, death or other things to where at the end the protagonist is left alone or almost alone to face the antagonist on their own. This is also the moment where the protagonist starts to gain some success in their try-fail cycle efforts. Where small successes bolster the protagonist's determination and they begin to make headway against the antagonist as the antagonist ups the ante. This is also the point where the protagonist starts to gain some of the previously battered self-image back. But they can't go in guns blazing just yet. This recovery needs to be slow and fraught with trial and trouble. Each victory in this process of moving from mid point to plot point 2 in this section of the book needs to be hard fought and hard won. This is where the warrior part of the character arc becomes evident.

Remember, the reader doesn't want it to be easy. There's no such thing as handing your protagonist some duct tape and telling him to go fix it. (Or you're going to get book throwing and hate mail or at least bad reviews.) This is the point where they have to find it in themselves and win the race and defeat the bad guys on their own and with their wits and intelligence. This is where in a horror, suspense, mystery, thriller the danger is very real and the antagonist is playing all their cards to win. We're not just seeing one pinch point or reminder of the bad guys, we're seeing numerous points where the antagonist is trying to undo the progress the protagonist made.

In a romance, this is where the protagonist and the love interest realize they really like each other and all heaven and hell are combining to stop it. The struggle needs to be real, believable, and emotionally resonant with the reader. Make the reader cheer out loud and clutch the book to their chest after they close the back cover.

So at this point on your cards you should be planning scenes that take us through mid point, and into the climax of the story. Again, don't worry about numbering them just yet and if you are color-coding them this is a good time to do that. The cards should be reflecting both the protagonist's plan of attack and the antagonist stepping up their efforts to make the protagonist fail.

This is also where the stakes rise sometimes at an alarming rate. The task at hand seems to be impossible to overcome and we are making the reader cringe and want to stop reading because of the intensity, but they can't put it down because they HAVE to see how it ends. This is where your reader becomes a fan. This is where in the realm of character arc the protagonist goes from being the wanderer to becoming the warrior.

In Latent, the mid point is the events leading up to the revelation of the O-code tattoo on his victim, Maiko and himself. Representing the depth of betrayal of Damashii Enterprises, and a loss of control, time, and or consciousness somewhere in his life where he doesn't remember getting the tattoo. It also sets up Damashii as something more sinister than just a corporation that employs a hit man for revenge purposes.

Plot point two is the climax of the story. This is the epic car chase scene, the final battle. This is where the protagonist and antagonist finally have the face to face and the battle is won. Whether by the protagonist or antagonist doesn't matter. Sometimes the protagonist fails and the antagonist wins. And the protagonist then slinks away in defeat.

Don't think this is a bad thing. For the reader, this is a very emotional scene. The reader is totally emotionally engaged with the protagonist in the struggle and the pain for the protagonist is a very real emotional resonation.

This is the point in the story where it has gone from approximately halfway through the book to three-quarters of the book. Remember the number isn't important as the feel. And it's okay to have a longer or shorter active stage as the story demands. I am a firm believer that too many restrictions and guidelines squashes creativity and to either add in blather or taking something out because you need to hit a specific number of pages in the story and makes the story flat. Just, remember, these parts of the story are a guideline, not an exact number.

If anyone tells you otherwise they are in my opinion,
looking at structure too analytically and not enough of it as an
art form. Realizing that its art (and yes art has some rules, but
it's not logic based like math and science) is where that
"drafting but knowing where you're going" freedom that
most authors seek is found. It's their Valhalla.

In Latent, plot point two is where Antony's character arc
conflict, (the religious conflict and war on himself by himself)
collides with the story plot which is his hits and his work for
Damashii. It's the scene where Maiko gives him the
assignment to kill Sori Katsu. Not only a religious person and
someone prominent in his wife Elite's life, but a man he
knows is innocent just like Kyo Yoji, a man he killed earlier.
That moment of conflict and his choice to refuse the hit and
then his choices to detain Maiko and her driver, and for he
and Elite to disappear is the moment where he changes,
where he starts to resolve the conflict and moves from a
warrior to a hero.

So a few things about plot point two before we move
forward. After PP2 there can be no new information given or
no new characters. (Granted reflection, (sequel) might reveal
some info, but it pertains to the resolution.)

As far as character arc goes, this is where the protagonist
moves from warrior to hero. This is where they defeat the
antagonist (usually) and save the world. This moment is when
after the fires are put out, and the protagonist stands up and
brushes themselves off. The protagonist is reunited with their
allies and wounds are bandaged.

The world wants and needs to return to normal. Because we as readers and humans crave routine and normalcy. Sometimes the general public is aware of the battle that happened, sometimes they are oblivious.

This is when the protagonist also chooses to either be a braggart about their accomplishments or simply walk away and try to live in that normal world they had before although that can't happen for them because they no longer belong to that normal world. Even if everyone around them still does. This is one reason why in some resolutions, the hero seeks out a life of solitary reflection or periods of meditative silence. This is also sometimes where the protagonist drops the hero stereotype and becomes a mentor to a new orphan turned warrior in training.

In that last riding off into the sunset scene of the book. The ending needs to be emotionally satisfying. Regardless of who won the battle.

In horror, the sun is figuratively coming over the horizon and the monsters are gone. In a mystery the crime is solved, the antagonist is punished and the victim gets justice. In thriller and suspense the threat is gone and the world is resuming daily life, in a romance, the two love interests are together and happy for at least the moment and the antagonist is defeated.

In Latent Antony has exacted revenge for the events in PP2, but it comes at a terrible price. He is left alone, directionless and suicidal. But a small side character offers him an alternative that is tempting.

In the resolution stage, you need to wrap everything up that you've presented as an issue, so keep that in mind as you present the scenes that happen coming into PP2. If you keep adding elements and details to deal with, you're going to have to fix them in the end. And who wants a huge resolution stage? Most readers don't. They want something satisfactory, but also more short and sweet than drawn out.

In a stand-alone, all loose ends must be resolved in the PP2 moment or in resolution. This is a good reason to keep your subplots to a manageable level and all of the pinch and try-fail cycles need to pertain to the story plot or character arc. And why it's definitely a good idea to watch how many divergent details you add into the story. I know most of us authors have a million ideas. It's okay to keep some of them for another story. Although you should write book one as a standalone so if the rest doesn't get picked up the reader still has a satisfactory ending. (Granted, with self-publishing nowadays, you can still finish a series that gets dropped. But that is a whole nother story) A few loose ends may be left undone to make the reader think, but they must be small and insignificant in regards to the main plot and arcs.

If this story is a part of a series, then you need address those "story only" issues to tie up. It will be necessary for you to leave some things unresolved but they must pertain to the overall series character and plot arc. However, you can leave over series plot, character arc, and conflict open.

If a character is leaving the series, their arc must be

resolved. If a new character is being introduced, their arc must be presented. If the antagonistic force in the book is unique to that book, it must be resolved. If the antagonistic arc is series wide it can be left unfinished but should be addressed and the stakes and risks should be increased. If the antagonist gets away, there must be a reasonable explanation. There sometimes is a larger antagonist that the smaller antagonist is working for, or is part of.

The protagonist needs to have learned enough to face the next books trouble but can't be all powerful. At least not yet. The lessons learned need to be good but not all-encompassing. They still need some flaws and quirks. Even if they have won the battle, there's still the war to fight.

Often times, scars from the first book come roaring back into the protagonist's life at the worst times and shocks the reader and the protagonist as to what happened and why it is bothering them.

If you are writing a series you should be thinking ahead at least one book, if not the whole series. You should have a clear idea of the protagonist, antagonist and plot arc for the whole series before you hit send on a submission for book one. It's not a bad idea to have a second set of cards detailing out the character, and plot arc for the series and refer to them often.

Now, how to put these cards and the story together. This is where you need a large table open piece of wall or someplace to set out all of the outlined scenes. So start laying out the cards in whatever order makes the most sense to you. Linear, block style columns, or however seems right. Place what you know is the beginning in one place and the ending where the ending should be. Then start placing the plot points in the ¼ ½ ¾ places.

Have a spot set aside for note cards that are notes only. Like events foreshadowing and elements needed in the story.

Now that you have a very basic recipe set out you can start to add the scenes into that story timeline where they are needed. Once the cards are laid out you can go back and read through them and see if everything is in the right place. This is why a table and no numbers on the cards makes this an easy process. This way you can move things around and rearrange scenes that you as the author thought might have been great in one place but are even better in another.

When all of the rearranging is done then is the time to number the cards. Especially if the cards might get dropped or jumbled in a bag. Some authors punch holes in them and tie them together or use a ring of sorts.

I myself transfer the scenes, and notes into a computer document and go from there.

At this point, I do something different with my "scene list/outline". Each scene for me becomes a chapter. (Sometimes the scene is too big and I actually break a scene into two or more chapters to make the chapters smaller and easier to read.) Then, I give the chapter or scene a name even if I don't use the chapter name in the book. Second, I write a short one to two sentence synopsis of what happens in the scene. Third, I write the plot and character arc significance of that scene/chapter. If there's no significance and it doesn't move the plot or character arc forward, I either change something in the scene to make it move the story or I delete it.

An example of what a scene entry in my master chapter outline looks like is this:

1 Blood

Intro Antony as assassin, coming home to wife, introduces religious conflict. Antony is in an industrial kitchen and makes a hit. He heads home, and at the train station, exchanges words with a street preacher telling the preacher his atheist views. He gets on the train.

Ordinary World, Introduction, hook.

At this point in time, I am ready to sit down and start drafting the story. One note: I either title my chapter or just type the word chapter, I still don't number them. Not until the LAST revision and edit round. There's still a chance I might move a chapter. And renumbering, if you move a chapter, is a huge pain in the butt.

I keep a hard copy of those notes right next to me as I draft. This way I know exactly what needs to happen in the scene as I let my characters discover what they are doing in such a scene. I make notes on it, I change scenes sometimes. I even move chapters around again if needed. When it comes to revision and editing it makes my work so much easier. If I need to move, add a scene or, delete something I make a notation on my hard copy or cards and keep it for later use. If I change something in the draft itself I also make a notation of it and I occasionally revise that document.

I also do a color highlight on the hard copy document to give me an idea how balanced it is in regards to varying characters POV, and antagonist scenes as opposed to protagonist, and subplot scenes.

When the draft and revisions are done I copy paste the document into another document and remove the titles, and the plot reasons and I have a very basic story outline that with some work and revision becomes a great synopsis.

Remember this?

1 Blood

Intro Antony as assassin, coming home to wife, introduces religious conflict. Antony is in an industrial kitchen and makes a hit. He heads home, and at the train station, exchanges words with a street preacher telling the preacher his atheist views. He gets on the train. Ordinary World Introduction, hook.

It now looks like this:

Antony is in an industrial kitchen and makes a hit. He heads home, and at the train station, exchanges words with a street preacher telling the preacher his atheist views. He gets on the train.

Outline and structure might sound intimidating but it can be easy to learn and use, and it is a great tool for drafting and revising a manuscript.

I hope this will help you outline and structure your story.

Now comes the fun part!

Planning your novel! Follow the prompts

and enjoy. Remember to reference the earlier information if you get stuck or lost. This is a workbook. The blank pages are for you to workshop on. Fill it up and make it personalized.

Book Title and Cover Page: This is where creativity and having fun becomes your inspiration. Have fun, create the cover of your dreams and use it to inspire you.

Book planning:
Book name:

Genre:

Ideas:

Theme:

Concept:

Premise:

Subplots:

Introduction of theme: (hook)

Ending:

Book planning:
Story Structure: (plot and timeline)

Part one - Introduction:

Theme introduction:

Plot Point #1:

Part two - Reactive Stage:

Pinch Point #1:

Mid Point:

Part three - Proactive Stage:

Pinch Point #2:

Plot Point #2:

Part four - Resolution:

STORY STRUCTURE & MASTER CHAPTER OUTLINE WORKBOOK

This is how I draw the whole story out on the board for my in-person students.

1) Introduction _____Reactive _____ Active _____ Resolution

2) Orphan _____Wanderer_____Warrior _____ Martyr

3) Beginning_____^_____*_____^_____*_____^_____End

4) Plot Point 1 _____Mid Point _____ Plot Point 2 (Represented by ^)

5) Pinch Point 1_____Pinch Point 2 (represented by *)

One note:

Everything above the #3 line is about CHARACTER and creates resonance between reader and characters.

Everything below the #3 line is PLOT and drives the story.

Structure Notes:

Structure Notes:

Structure Notes:

Structure Notes:

Characters:

A lot of character sections in other books have this extensive list of basic information for your character. Hair and eye color, parents, height and build. If you have a great list or find one, that is great. I feel that the list limited me and while I knew what the character looked like, I had no idea who they really were. Instead, I dug deep and really got into the character. Of course, I include the what, but I dig into the why and when did the why happen. What is his favorite breakfast cereal, even if the reader never gets that info. (Frosted Flakes BTW) Whether he wears boxers or goes commando. (No, I'm not telling you.) What does he fear? (Attention) If given something valuable, what would he do to keep or protect it? (Anything)

Dig deep. Paste pictures in, interview them. Make the character live on the page.

Character:

Character:

Character:

Character:

Character:

Character:

Character:

Setting:

What is your world like? Earth? A fantasy world? Past? Future?

Again, dig deep, what is the world like on the surface as well as what is under the surface, and what does the world look like from above? Draw, paste in pictures, make the setting as well rounded as the characters.

Setting:

Setting:

Maps, Diagrams, Drawings:

Maps, Diagrams, Drawings:

Maps, Diagrams, Drawings:

Maps, Diagrams, Drawings:

Maps, Diagrams, Drawings:

Story details: (Notes that need to be known but not necessarily written into the story.)

Story details:

Story details:

Story details:

Scene list: (list what scenes you want, or "see" in the book, keep track of what you have used and what is still available.)

Scene list:

Scene list:

Scene list:

Scene list:

Chapter outline: (structure notations, chapter number, plot reasons for scene, short 2-3 sentence synopsis of chapter)

MCO:

MCO:

MCO:

MCO:

Writing Progress Chart: (date started, number of pages per day, notes)

Writing Progress Chart:

Writing Progress Chart:

Writing Progress Chart:

Editing Checklist: (Make sure you've put it away for at least a few days if not weeks)

Read the MS for grammar, spelling, and typos (often times this phase is easier if you print the MS on paper)

Read the MS out loud for repeated words and confusing scenes, paragraphs, and sentences

Read the MS for character details (all characters are deep and thought out, descriptions are consistent, internal dialogue/emotions present, characters are consistent and complicated (no mary janes or supermen) dialogue is consistent)

Read the MS for setting details (details are consistent, no purple prose descriptions, descriptions are short but well done, setting mimics mood and emotions of scene)

Read the MS for voice, pacing, and tension (Is the voice present and not overbearing? Make sure the timeline is compact, and chapters work together, each chapter has a plot purpose and moves the story along, can you combine scenes? Or split large chapters?)

Read the MS for plot (Is there an overall plot arc through the story? Does the protagonist, secondary characters, and antagonist have an arc? Do the characters have motivation? Are you following Structure? Does each chapter also have an arc? Are your try/fail cycles believable? Do you have more than one line of plot/problem, are they interwoven and complex but not too complicated?)

Read the MS for thematic details (Do you have subtle well-placed clues and secrets placed throughout the story?

Are there subtle repeated themes and patterns in the MS? Do you have myths and archetypes? Do you have enough backstory, is it short and sweet? Are you sure your backstory is not overwhelming? Do you have real-world relevance, so your reader connects with the MS?

Send it out to beta readers. (Grow a thick skin, nonfamily, willing to be honest and critical. Remember you don't have to change everything a beta says, it is your baby after all. But, often times they have good things to say.)

Editing Notes:

Editing Notes:

Editing Notes:

Editing Notes:

Editing Notes:

Synopsis:

Synopsis:

Synopsis:

Book Blurb/Back Cover Copy:

Book Blurb:

Query letter:

Query Letter:

Query Letter:

Submissions Ledger: (date, submitted to who, partial, full, rejected, notes)

Submissions Ledger:

Submissions Ledger:

Submissions Ledger:

Special Book Events: (The date you started the
book, date rough draft finished, date started editing,
date submitted and where etc.)

Special Book Events:

My writing goals:

My writing goals:

Monthly goal list:

Month 1:

Month 2:

Month 3:

Month 4:

Month 5:

Month 6:

Month 7:

Month 8:

Month 9:

Month 10:

Month 11:

Month 12:

Other Notes:

STORY STRUCTURE & MASTER CHAPTER
OUTLINE WORKBOOK

STORY STRUCTURE & MASTER CHAPTER
OUTLINE WORKBOOK

STORY STRUCTURE & MASTER CHAPTER OUTLINE WORKBOOK

C. MICHELLE JEFFERIES

STORY STRUCTURE & MASTER CHAPTER
OUTLINE WORKBOOK

STORY STRUCTURE & MASTER CHAPTER OUTLINE WORKBOOK

STORY STRUCTURE & MASTER CHAPTER
OUTLINE WORKBOOK

STORY STRUCTURE & MASTER CHAPTER
OUTLINE WORKBOOK

STORY STRUCTURE & MASTER CHAPTER
OUTLINE WORKBOOK

STORY STRUCTURE & MASTER CHAPTER
OUTLINE WORKBOOK

About The Author

C. Michelle Jefferies is a writer who believes that the way to examine our souls is to explore the deep and dark as well as the shallow. To manipulate words in a way that makes a person think and maybe even second guess. Her worlds include suspense, urban fantasy, and an occasional twist of steampunk. When she is not writing, she can be found on the yoga mat, hand binding journals, dyeing cloth, and serving ginger tea. The author and creator divides her time between stories, projects, and mothering four of her seven children on the wild and windy plains of Wyoming.

Find C. Michelle Jefferies on the web!
cmichellejefferies.wordpress.com
facebook.com/CMichelleJefferiesAuthor
twitter.com/cmichellejeffe1
pinterest.com/cmjefferies

Acknowledgements

Thank you to my Tooele Writers group who encouraged the development of this book. My writing class students who were my guinea pigs on the early versions. And Elizabeth and Levi Mueller who helped me when I lost a big section of this book into the cyber aether. To my family who puts up with hours of me working, and my ever lovable hubby who supports me in this writing madness.

Made in the USA
Columbia, SC
19 April 2018